# Kids Connect

PIONEER EDITION

By Kent Page, Terrell Smith, and Peter Winkler

CONTENTS

The sun is not up in Peshawar. It is a city in Pakistan. Loudspeakers call from a mosque (MAHSK), or Muslim house of worship. They call people to come pray. They say, "God is great! It is better to pray than sleep! Come to prayers!"

Ten-year-old Garana gets up from a mat. She sleeps on the floor of her family's house. She puts on her black robe. She puts an old shawl on her head. Then she walks to the mosque to pray.

Garana and her family have lived in their one-room house for several years. Their house is in a **refugee** camp. There are about 50,000 Afghan refugees in the camp. They are people who have left Afghanistan because of war or drought.

Garana works hard. Her father left the family a few years ago. Her mother can't see very well. So her mother can't help very much. Her older brother makes carpets all day. Her younger brother is too small to help much. So Garana does most of the housework. But her day is not all work. She has time for school. She even has time for a little fun.

A day in the life of a young Afghan refugee

# Garana's Story

BY KENT PAGE

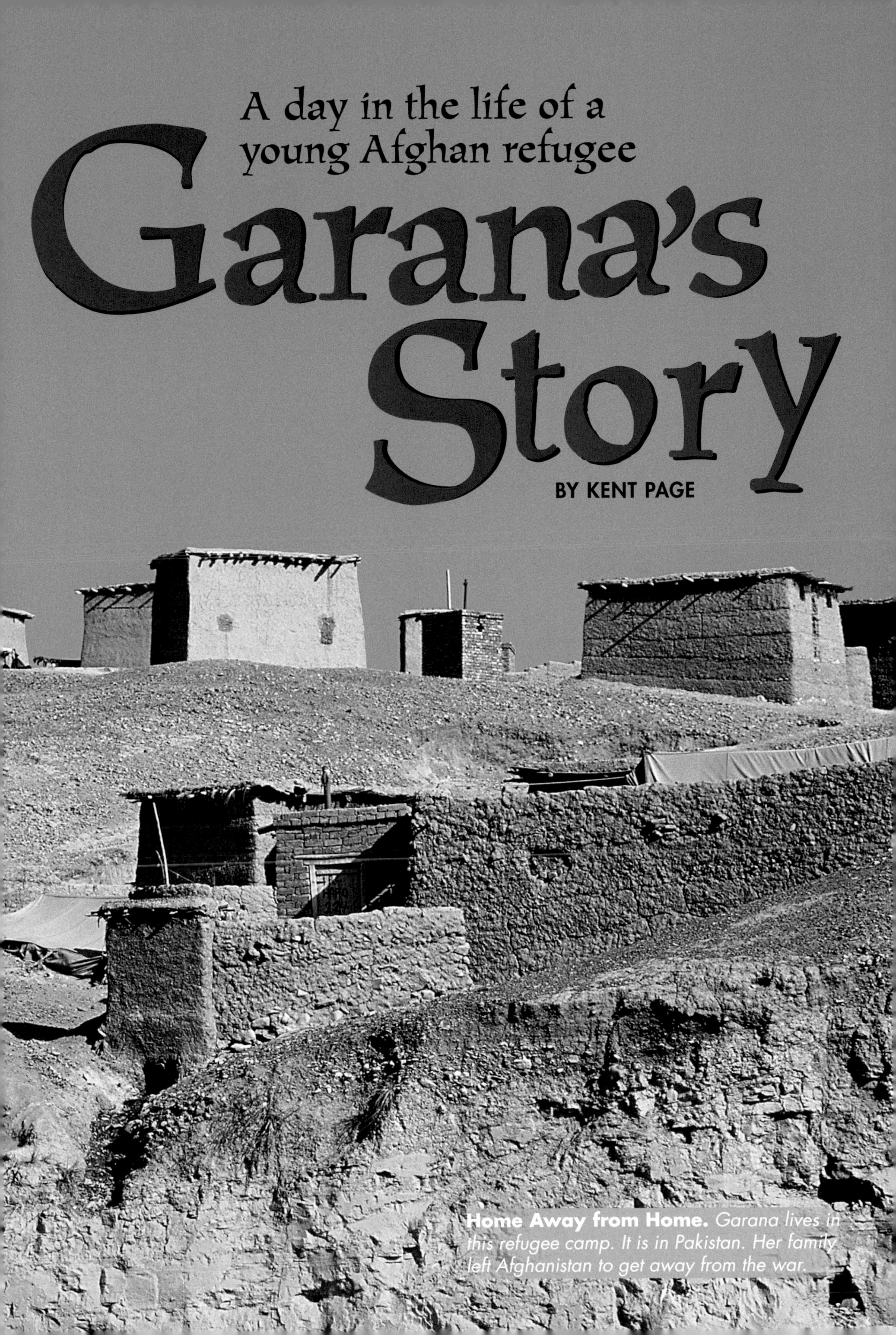

**Home Away from Home.** *Garana lives in this refugee camp. It is in Pakistan. Her family left Afghanistan to get away from the war.*

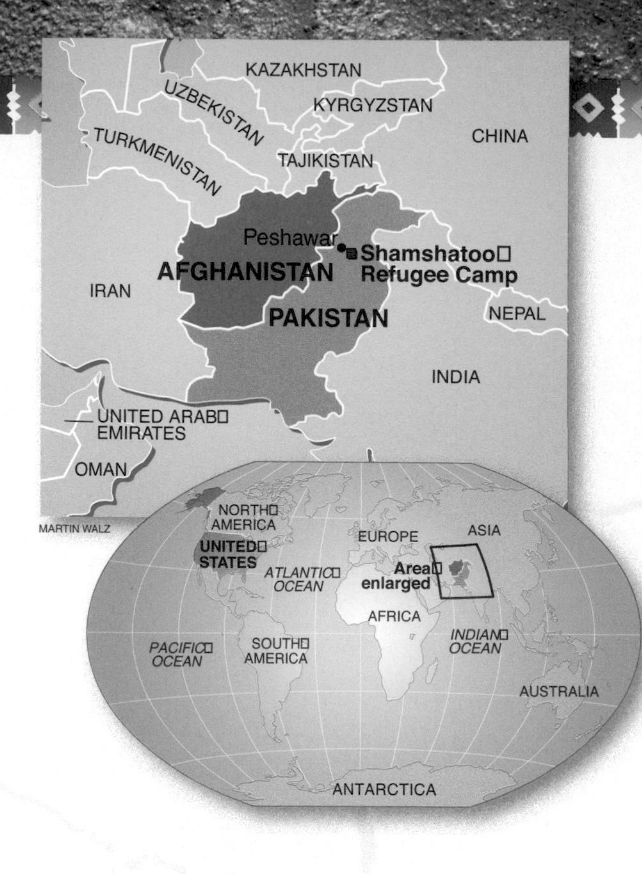


**Heavy Work.** *Garana gets water five or six times a day. She works hard to pump the handle up and down.*

**Follow the Letters.** *Garana and her teacher practice the English alphabet.*

## Early Morning

Garana begins her morning chores after prayers. She walks to the water pump. She fills two bottles. Then she goes home. She eats bread with hot tea for breakfast. Then she goes to the backyard. Next she sweeps the floor.

Then she walks to the bakery. She leaves some flour. The bakers use it to make bread. Garana's family will eat that bread for their next three meals. Now it's time to walk to school.

## Class Time

Ten-year-old Garana is in first grade. When she lived in Afghanistan, girls were not allowed to go to school. She has to work hard to catch up.

Garana gets to school at 8:30. Boys and girls are in different classes. There are thirty-five girls in Garana's class. The students sit on the floor. They study math. They study the Afghan languages. They study the English alphabet. The class also sings and draws. Garana likes school.

**Bread Bakers.** *Garana takes flour to the bakery every day. The bakers make bread for her family.*

"My favorite subject is English," she says. "If you can speak languages, then you can understand what people say. It's easier to get things done."

Today Garana stands at the chalkboard. She helps the class learn the English alphabet.

## Lunch Break

Classes end before lunch. The students run to the playground. They play on the swings. They play on the slide. They play on the merry-go-round. Garana likes to play with her friends. But soon it's time for more chores.

She goes to the bakery. She picks up the bread. Then she walks back to her house. She says hello to her mother. Then Garana goes to the pump to get water. When she returns, she makes tea. Garana sits on her mat and eats lunch. Today her mother made potatoes.

"Some days we have potatoes. Some days we have rice. And some days we have beans," Garana says. "Whatever we eat for lunch, we have it again for dinner. Rice is my favorite food."

## Afternoon and Evening

After lunch, Garana goes back to the pump for water. She washes the plates and cups. Then she sweeps the house. She cleans the yard. She feeds the family's four chickens. If there is money, she buys food at the store. She does her homework after her chores.

Soon it's time for dinner. The refugee camp does not have electricity. So the family eats dinner before it gets dark. If any daylight is left, Garana plays with her best friend. Her name is Assia.

## A Wish for Peace

Garana has a hard life in the refugee camp. But at least there is no fighting. “I would like to go back home,” she says. “But not until there is **peace** everywhere. We are told at school that some parts of Afghanistan are safe. But there is fighting in other parts.”

Many share Garana’s wish. For more than 30 years, Afghanistan has suffered from war. Now Afghans, with help from many countries, are trying to make changes. They hope to bring peace to their country.

## Wordwise

**attend:** to go to a place regularly

**donate:** to give as a gift

**peace:** when there is no war or suffering

**refugee:** a person forced to leave home and go to live in another country

**High Hopes.** *Garana and Assia (in pink shirt) hope to return to the mountains of Afghanistan.*

# Back to School

## Education = Hope for Afghan Children

By Terrell Smith

It was March 25, 2002. Crowds of children gathered throughout Afghanistan. Excited whispers filled the air. It's the first day of school!

These Afghan children were really happy to start school. Many hadn't **attended** school in years.

Without schools, many Afghan children grew up without the skills they needed to earn a living. For them, school equals hope.

**Ready to Learn.** *Afghan students hold new school supplies. The supplies were donated by students in the United States.*

### Class Acts

Unfortunately, many Afghan schools. were damaged by war. No one had money or materials to fix them.

So the United Nations Children's Fund (UNICEF) and the American Red Cross helped. They repaired the schools. They also bought new desks, chairs, chalkboards, and textbooks.

U.S. students helped, too. They **donated** money for school supplies. Afghan students got pencils, chalk, crayons, notebooks, rulers, jump ropes, and soccer balls.

### No Complaints

All this help was just a start. Afghan schools are still crowded. To make more room, most schools have two shifts. Half the children attend classes in the morning. The other half go to school in the afternoon. But Afghan students aren't complaining. They're just glad to be back.

"I never stopped thinking about the day when I might go back to school," says Safi, a nine-year-old girl. "When I heard that school would start again, I was so happy."

# Making Fri

By Peter Winkler

**"Enemies" learn and play together at Israel's Hand in Hand School. Can they teach their parents how to live in peace?**

Each morning in Israel, 300 kids do something amazing. They go to school. What's the big deal? Their schools mix Palestinians and Jews peacefully. The two groups have fought for decades. Violence has torn the country apart.

Jews and Palestinians live in different areas. They rarely meet. They don't use the same language. They don't share a religion. Their children go to different schools.

**Bridging** such differences seems impossible. But two friends have decided to try.

**Who's Who?** *One of these students is Palestinian. The other two are Jewish. Yet they laugh together like any group of friends.*

ends

## Mission Impossible?

Lee Gordon is Jewish. Amin Khalaf is Palestinian. They met in 1996. They formed an **organization** called Hand in Hand. They build schools where Palestinians and Jews can be friends and classmates. What's it like to go to a school like this? Let's find out.

## Learning Shalom

School starts at 7:30 a.m. Students walk through a metal gate. Safety is important in Israel.

One morning a teacher was late. She was crying and shaking. She was driving to work. She saw a bus explode.

Such events let students and teachers know that their school is important. "When something gets bombed, we talk about it in class," says a Palestinian student. They talk about better ways to solve problems.

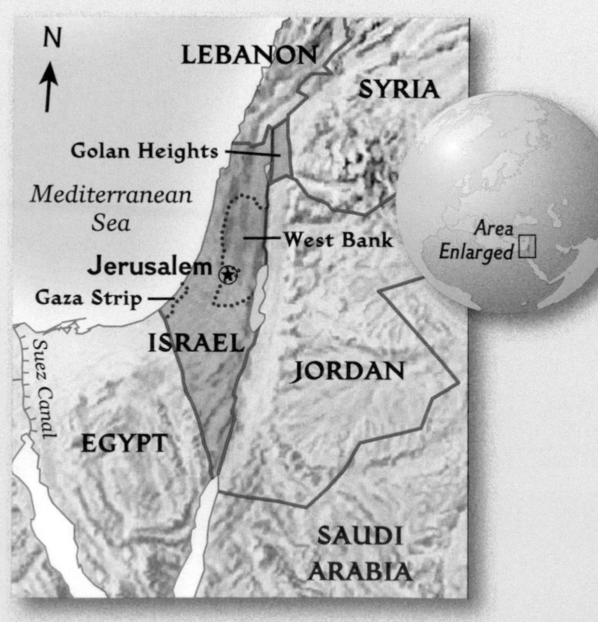

**Teaching by Example.** *A Palestinian teacher talks with students. Jewish and Palestinian teachers work together at the Hand in Hand Schools.*

"If there were more schools like this," explains a Jewish friend, "more children would learn shalom [peace]. They would grow up to be peaceful."

## Speaking My Language

It's 8:15 a.m. Time to start class. About half the students are Jewish. They speak Hebrew. The other half are Palestinians. They speak Arabic.

So, at Hand in Hand Schools each class has two teachers. They plan lessons together. One speaks in Arabic. One speaks in Hebrew. But they never translate, or explain, what the other is saying. Kids must listen in both languages. It's not easy.

**Busy Street.** *Palestinian kids watch soldiers guarding a street.*

But students learn quickly. By third grade, most are **bilingual**. That means they know two languages

## Bridging Differences

Classes end at 1:30 p.m. Everyone is ready for lunch. Everybody eats at school. The cooks follow food-related rules from the students' religions.

Lunch is over. Now it's activity time. Kids can try karate or yoga. They can play soccer or practice music. They can design books.

Relaxed times are important. Through activities, students learn to see each other as ordinary people. They form friendships that bridge real, deep differences.

School ends at 3:30 p.m. The kids head home. There the students become teachers.

## Home Schooling

Like kids everywhere, Hand in Hand students bring friends home. Those friends may be the first Jews or Palestinians the rest of the family ever gets to know. Having an "enemy" in the house is uncomfortable at first. But soon, people are eating together. They are talking together. They are playing together. One friendship at a time, they're learning shalom.

### Wordwise

**bilingual:** able to use two languages

**bridge:** to make connections between

**organization:** an official group that works for a common goal

# Make a Difference!

**Read about the ways kids connect with others. Then answer these questions.**

1. What does Garana do around the house to help her family?
2. Why does Garana like learning English?
3. How have students in the U.S. helped students in Afghanistan?
4. How do teachers in the Hand in Hand School work together?
5. What do Hand in Hand School students do after classes? How does the author present the events that take place at school?